CONNECTIONS

After Juliet
Sharman Macdonald

Born in Glasgow, Sharman Macdonald became an actress on graduation from Edinburgh University but gave it up in order to write. Her first play, *When I Was a Girl I Used to Scream and Shout*, won her the Evening Standard Award for Most Promising Playwright of 1984 and ran in London for one year. Her other plays include *When We Were Women*, *The Winter Guest* (which was also made into a film), *Borders of Paradise* and *Sea Urchins*. *Wild Flowers*, a filmscript, was made for Channel Four. Her novels *The Beast* and *Night, Night* have been published by Collins.

CONNECTIONS

After Juliet

SHARMAN MACDONALD

faber and faber

STANLEY
THORNES

First published in this edition 2001
by Faber and Faber Limited
3 Queen Square London WC1N 3AU
Published in the United States by Faber and Faber, Inc.,
an affiliate of Farrar, Straus and Giroux, New York
After Juliet was first published in *New Connections 99* in 1999

Typeset by Country Setting, Kingsdown, Kent CT14 8ES
Printed in England by Mackays of Chatham plc, Chatham, Kent

A CIP record for this book
is available from the British Library

ISBN 0–571–20614–X (Faber edn)
ISBN 0–7487–4288–3 (Stanley Thornes edn)

2 4 6 8 10 9 7 5 3 1

Contents

Foreword

The plays in this series were generated through a unique
and epic project initiated by the Royal National Theatre,
London, and funded by BT.

For many years the Education Department at the RNT
had been receiving calls from youth theatre companies
and schools asking us to recommend scripts for them
to perform. They were looking for contemporary,
sophisticated, unpatronising scripts with great plots and
storylines, where the characters would fit the age range
of the young people playing them. At that time, there
weren't many plays written for the 11-to-19 age group.
So we decided to approach the best writing talent around
and ask them to write short plays specifically for young
people.

In two-year cycles over a period of six years, we
created a portfolio of new plays and invited 150 schools
and youth theatres to choose the one that most excited
them. We then invited the participants to come on a
weekend retreat and work through the script with the
writer before producing the play in their home venue.
Some of those productions were then invited to one of
ten festivals at professional theatres throughout the UK.
Each two-year cycle culminated in a summer festival at
the Royal National Theatre, where the stages, back-stage
areas and foyers were ablaze with youthful energy and
creativity.

But the story doesn't end there. As we've discovered,
the UK isn't alone in demanding fantastic new scripts for
the youth market. A fourth cycle is already under way,
and this time the portfolio will include more contributions

from overseas. As long as there's a need, we will continue
to commission challenging work to feed the intelligence,
imagination and ingenuity of young people and the
adults with whom they work.

Suzy Graham-Adriani
Royal National Theatre
July 2000

For more information on the writers and the work
involved on the BT/National Connections project, visit:
www.nt-online.org

AFTER JULIET

Sharman Macdonald

based on an original idea by Keira Knightley
with thanks to William Shakespeare

Characters

Benvolio
A Montague. Sixteen. Romeo's best friend.

Valentine
A Montague. Sixteen. Mercutio's twin brother.

Rosaline
A Capulet. Fifteen. Juliet's cousin.

Bianca
A Capulet. Fourteen but younger than her years.
Suffers from *petit mal*. Juliet's cousin.

Helena
A Capulet. Sixteen. Bianca's sister. Juliet's cousin.

Rhona
A Capulet. Sixteen. A visitor from Glasgow.
Juliet's cousin. Plays the flute (or another silver
solo wind instrument. A tin whistle would do).

Alice
A Capulet. Sixteen. Juliet's cousin.

Livia
A Capulet. Fourteen. Rosaline's half sister.
Juliet's cousin.

Angelica
A Capulet servant. Juliet's nurse. Thirty.

Lorenzo
A Capulet. Sixteen.

Gianni
A Capulet. Sixteen.

Petruchio
A Capulet. Eighteen. Tybalt's brother.

Romeo
A Montague. Dead.

Juliet
A Capulet. Dead.

The Drummer
Ever present. Non-partisan. A slight threat.
A small sense that he's a puppeteer. At times he cues
the action. This should be subtle; there and gone in the
flutter of an eyelash. The sentences that describe the
action are long: the action itself should be short.

A Musician

*The music is original; written by Caleb Knightley and
Adrian Howgate for sampler, drums and flute.*

One set.

*The quotations in the text are adapted from
Brooke's Romeus and Juliet (1562) which was,
in turn, a translation from the Italian of Bandello's
Romeus and Juliet (1554).*

*The text should be played at speed.
Should 'fuck' be a pain and a trouble
please change it to 'feck' or a rhythmic equivalent.*

*** or * in the text indicates that two pieces
of dialogue run simultaneously.*

Silence.
   The drummer alone.
   Stands.
   Moves.
   Drums. Rolling soft and long.
   Rosaline's idly throwing dice. Again and again and
again.
   The drummer click click clicks. Benvolio edges into
the sunshine. Gazes up at Rosaline's balcony.

Livia
   He's looking at you.
Rosaline
   Let him.
Livia
   Romeo's dead, Rosaline
   And didn't even think of you.
   Forgot you as soon as he saw Juliet.
Rosaline
   I can't turn my love off like a tap.
Livia
   Forget Romeo.
   He didn't know you loved him.
   You wouldn't speak to him.
   You sent his letters back;
   Left his flowers without water to die
   And his poems in the rain.
   In what land do you call that love?
Rosaline
   I wanted him to see

I wasn't so easily won.
He was a Montague after all.
'Never trust a Montague.'
I sucked that in with mother's milk.

Livia

Your mother!

Rosaline

My mother loved my father
Then your mother came along
And my father treated my mother with scorn
And traded her in for
A somewhat younger woman.
Don't talk to me about caution with men.
I learnt from observation
That what's most hard come by is most valued.

Livia

If I were a man I'd look for a woman to keep me
If I were that way inclined
Or a man if no woman could be found.
There's no intrinsic honour in work
Only stress sweat and labour.
Whatever the gender.
Not to do it
That's what I'm after.
Marry. Marry money, Rosaline.
Hire a cook for the kitchen
A nanny for the children
And unless he's very talented in that direction
Hire a mistress for the bedroom.
** Time would never hang heavy on my hands.
For I can live quite happily with my female friends.

The drummer click, click, clicks and points at
Rosaline. **

Recorded words. An announcement. Coming from
afar. Coming close. Moving on. Moving away.

PA
'Both households straight are charged on payne of
  losing lyfe
Theyr bloudy weapons to lay aside; to cease the
  styrred stryfe.
The wiser sort Prince Escalus calls to councell streyt
That a trial may be held in front of the populace
And justice meted out to those elders of this place
Judged to blame for the deaths of Romeo and Juliet.
  Angelica the nurse stands accused
The servant Peter.
Fryr Lawrence.
The apothecary of Mantua.
  Both households straight are charged on payne of
  losing lyfe
Theyr bloudy weapons to lay aside; to cease the
  styrred stryfe.'

** *Rosaline climbs down and moves swiftly through
the piazza.*
  *Valentine slides out of the shadows. Catches hold of
her. Holds her tightly by the wrist.*

Rosaline
Is this how you keep the truce? *
Valentine
There's no knife at your throat.
Rosaline
* Tybalt sported with your brother;
Cat and mouse.
Romeo killed Mercutio
Who stepped between.
Ask Benvolio.
All who were there say so.
I say it who loved Romeo.
Valentine
I see a spitting cat

In your eyes, Rosaline.
I don't see a truce.

Rosaline
You must like my sleeve very much
To hold on to it for so long.

Valentine
Benvolio watches you day and night.

Rosaline
So where is he now
When I need him?

Valentine
Leave him alone, Rosaline.
Don't smile at him.
Don't stop when you see him.
Don't, knowing he's watching
Wash in the sunlight
With the shutters open.
No girl's tricks.
I know them all.
Don't rouge your cheeks for him.
Nor wear perfume for him.
If you do any of these things
I will see.
I will know.
I will come for you.
With no Prince of Cats
Your rabble won't protect you.

Rosaline
We elect a new Prince tonight.
Keep clear, Valentine.
Lest you get scratched.

Valentine
Know what I want right now?

Rosaline
A dress like mine?

Valentine
  Wash my hands of you
  That's what I want. **
  Get the smell of you and all Capulets
  Off my hands.
Rosaline
  ** You want your Mammy, Valentine, like all the wee
  bully boys.

  Lorenzo and Gianni slide out of the shadows.
    Begin to close on Valentine.

  Go Valentine. Go.
  Don't be a fool.
  This is our territory.

  He lets her go. Ostentatiously spits on his hands and
  *wipes them on his tunic. ***
    This could be Verona.
    Or it could be Edinburgh, Dublin, New York or
  Liverpool.
    Narrow alleys. High buildings almost touching at
  the top. A strip of blue sky shading into cloud far
  away. Heat. The sudden space of a piazza.
    *** The boys slide away. Melt.*
    Rosaline runs.
    The girls on balconies. Like a thought murmuring.

Bianca
  ** Clouds coming.
Alice
  Rain on its way.
Livia
  Thunder.
Rhona
  Close.
Rosaline
  August.

Helena
Muggy.
Bianca
Clouds coming in.

Distant thunder.
*** The girls murmur continues round and round,
under Gianni and Lorenzo, accompanied by music.
Almost a song. Until it fades and dies.*
*** Light hits the drummer and moves on to Gianni
and Lorenzo in the shadows.*

Gianni
D'you feel a breeze?
Lorenzo
Nah. You?
Gianni
Nah.
Lorenzo
The earth's holding its breath.
Gianni
What?
Lorenzo
Feels like.
Gianni
Feels like the earth's holding its breath?
Lorenzo
Feels like.
Gianni
Fuck off.
Lorenzo
Day like this. I made love.
Gianni
You did not.
Lorenzo
After the day. In the night. I did. I made love.

Gianni
  To a girl?
Lorenzo
  To a marmoset.
Gianni
  A marmoset?
Lorenzo
  To a girl. To a girl.
Gianni
  What girl? What fucking girl?
Lorenzo
  Juliet.
Gianni
  Fuck off.
Lorenzo
  Her name was Juliet.
Gianni
  You made love with Juliet! That's what you're telling
  me?
Lorenzo
  Juliet.
Gianni
  Juliet?
Lorenzo
  You're in my face, Gianni.
Gianni
  You made love with Juliet?
Lorenzo
  I made love with Juliet.
Gianni
  You had her.
Lorenzo
  I had her.
Gianni
  You did not.

Lorenzo
I know who I made love to.
Gianni
You're a big fuck-off liar, Lorenzo.
Lorenzo
You calling me a liar?
Gianni
A fuck-off, fucking liar.

Lorenzo gets his arm round Gianni's neck.

Lorenzo
Know what I call this? Do you know what I call this?
'Last Gasp' that's what I call this. Fucking last gasp.
   I'm fucking sharing something with you man.
You're my friend, and I'm sharing it with you.
Capulet to Capulet. Lorenzo to Gianni. I'm sharing a
treasured moment with my friend.
   I made love to Juliet. It was hot. I was thirteen. The
night before I was fourteen. She came to me.
   First she was babying me
   Like she was my mother
   Then she's wrestling me
   Like she was my friend.
   Then . . .
   She's my lover.
Gianni
Juliet?

The hold tightens.

Lorenzo
Juliet.

A beat. A thought.

Gianni
Juliet who?

A beat. A realisation.

Lorenzo
Shit, Gianni.
Shit, man.
Juliet!
Not that Juliet.
Juliet!
Gianni
Not that Juliet?
Lorenzo
Not that Juliet.
Gianni
Another Juliet?
Lorenzo
Another fucking Juliet.
Gianni
Common enough name.
Lorenzo
Common enough name.
Gianni
Easy fucking mistake.
Lorenzo
Easy fucking mistake.
Gianni
Not dead Juliet?
Lorenzo
Not dead fucking Juliet.

The hold's released.

Gianni
Too hot.
Lorenzo
Too fucking hot.
Gianni
You were thirteen?

Lorenzo
　Thirteen.
Gianni
　August you say?
Lorenzo
　It was hot.
　When we had our clothes off
　Lying there.
　The breeze cooled the sweat on her skin
　Her skin like ice
　Breeze like a kiss
　Kiss like silk
　Her skin was green in the moonlight.
Gianni
　Green?
Lorenzo
　Green.
Gianni
　Green skin?
Lorenzo
　Next day was August twelfth,
　St Lorenzo's Day,
　Open season.
　We came at them from above.
　They defended well.
　I was fourteen.
Gianni
　Good day.
Lorenzo
　Sweet good day.
Gianni
　Green skin?
Lorenzo
　Like she came to me
　From another world
　Another fucking world.

A clash of a cymbal. Music.
  Rosaline alone. Running. Dodging. Running.
  A stone's thrown. And another. And another.
  One hits her.
  She cowers down.
Benvolio comes up quietly behind her.
  Startles her.
Takes her under the arcade.

Rosaline
  I'm not frightened.
Benvolio
  No need now.
Rosaline
  Now you're with me?
Benvolio
  I came to talk to you.
Rosaline
  And your shadow?
Benvolio
  I'm on my own, Rosaline.
Rosaline
  Someone's throwing the stones.
Benvolio
  Some kid that's all. Not one of ours.
Rosaline
  Hardly one of ours.
Benvolio
  The truce is holding.
Rosaline
  It's a fine peace.
  A bruising peace.
  Prince Escalus's peace.
Benvolio
  It'll settle when the trial's over.
  The day's hot with the sweat of it.

Rosaline
When there's a new Prince of Cats.
Then the days will breath again.
Benvolio
You are frightened.
Rosaline
I'll conquer it.

Thunder rolls.

That was a long one.

Benvolio runs roaring at the shadows.
   Rosaline claps her hands over her ears. Laughing.

Benvolio
See anyone?
Rosaline
Was that entirely necessary?

He smiles.

Benvolio
You're safe.
Rosaline
With a Montague?
Benvolio
At your service.

Benvolio comes towards her.

You're shivering.
Rosaline
A goose walked over my grave.
Benvolio
Don't say that.

She sits down on the cobbles. Takes out a rollie.
Lights it.

These'll kill you.
Rosaline
A lot else in this world'll kill me faster.
Stones now.
Flung with a certain force
And on it's mark.
A stone'll kill you
Faster than tobacco.
Benvolio
Are you hurt?
Rosaline
What's a few bruises?

The sound of a flute.

I'm getting a crick in my neck.
Benvolio
Eh?
Rosaline
Sit down. I won't bite you.
Afraid I'll poison you if you get too close?

She looks at him.

Cat got your tongue?
Benvolio
What?
Rosaline
Don't look so sorrowful.

The flute haunts the shadows.
    Silence.

Pity.
Benvolio
What?
Rosaline
It's gone.

He grabs the rollie from her.

Hey.

He chucks it.

That's good tobacco.
I paid hard cash for that.
Doesn't grow on trees.
Not for me it doesn't.
   I bet you always wash your hands.
After.
Benvolio
  After?
Rosaline
  Touching a Capulet.
Benvolio
  Velvet your claws, Rosaline.
Rosaline
  Do you find it a strain?
Benvolio
  What?
Rosaline
  Being so decent?
Benvolio
  I love you.
Rosaline
  Good God, why?
Benvolio
  I always have.
Rosaline
  How can you love me?
  You don't know me.

She swirls up ready to leave him. He catches her hand.

Each day when I awoke
The sun shone

Because round a corner
I might see Romeo coming.
The days I didn't see him
Were lost days.
The surprise of him
Was what I lived for.
Who do you love, Benvolio?
Rosaline?
Don't you know?
Romeo took her away with him
When he crossed over
Into the far country.

Benvolio
Rosaline?

She hesitates a moment puzzled by his gentleness.
    The drummer clack clack clacks on the rim. Points
at Rosaline.
    She goes.
    Benvolio stares at the drummer.

Gianni
You see her again?
Lorenzo
Juliet?
Gianni
After that night?
Lorenzo
Never saw her again.
Gianni
That's sad man, Lorenzo.
Lorenzo
Love of my life.
Gianni
So fucking sad.

A cymbal's struck. Music.
Blackout
Shadow and light. Clouds and sun.
Bianca alone watching.
The vision.
Frozen figures. Their clothes are punk Elizabethan.
Reds and greens. Their makeup, slightly stylised.
The drummer cues these figures into movement.
Tick tick ticks on the drum sticks.
The figures move into slow life. Join hands.
A minuet on a sampler. Live drums. Rhona's
playing a lonely flute.
A line of dancers, partnering each other, moves in
unison. A sword comes from somewhere. It's thrown
and caught. Thrown and caught. Thrown. A girl
catches it. Draws it from its scabbard. Teases the
line leader into a fight. Draws blood from his cheek.
So that, provoked, he draws his sword in anger.
The greens line up behind the girl: the reds behind
the boy. Weapons are drawn.
Bianca's whimpering.
A cymbal.
Blackout.
Still figures in the shadows.

Bianca
Waking shadows come to visit me.

Bianca and Helena alone. Helena's basket's on the
ground.
The sun's in and out of the clouds.
Not till the drummer signals to her does she put her
arms round Bianca.

Helena
You're standing on your feet. Your eyes are wide open.

Bianca
  Come from sleep's country.
Helena
  What did they say?
Bianca
  Alice will wear her bridesmaid's dress
  At the election tonight.
Helena
  All the way from beyond
  They came to tell you that.
  They were fond.
Bianca
  I can't hear what else
  They came to say . . .
  They came . . .
  I can't hear . . .
Helena
  Blow. Blow them away. See.

*She blows. The figures move and become just people
going to market. Meeting. Passing. Going home.
Disappearing.*

  All gone, Bianca?
Bianca
  All gone.
Helena
  The clouds are gathering.

*Helena picks up her empty basket. Takes Bianca's
hand.*

Bianca
  I want to put a flower down.
Helena
  On the way back.
Bianca
  I want to put a flower down now.

Helena
I haven't got a flower.
Bianca
Give me a flower.
Helena
I haven't got one.

The drummer tick tick ticks with his drum sticks.

Bianca
I'm hot. Very, very hot.

Helena's watching the clouds.

Helena
The rain's coming.

She tugs at Bianca's hand. She's childlike, Bianca, but not a child.
Benvolio's moving to get a better view. Careful not to come out of the shadows of the arcade.

Bianca
Feel me.
I'm sweating.

She takes Helena's hand. Puts it to her forehead. Helena pats her cheek.

Can I take this off?
Can I?
Can I take this off?
I need . . . I need . . .
Helena
I haven't got an umbrella, Bianca. Move.
Bianca
Ohhhhhhhhh.
I can't manage the buttons,

My fingers won't . . .
My finger's on the buttons.
Helena
Come here.

Helena undoes the buttons for her.

Bianca
I need . . .
I need . . .
I'm itchy.
Helena
Scratch.
Bianca
I'm itchy inside.
I need . . .
I need . . .
Helena
What?
Bianca
Do you love me?
Helena
Of course.

Bianca puts her hands on Helena's face.

Bianca
Cross. Lines here. Shadows here.
Helena
Smooth them away.

*Helena shrugs Bianca's jacket free of her shoulders.
Tugs it down over her hands.*

Promise not to take any more off.
No stripping in the market place
With all the folk there for the trial.
They won't like you stripping.

Bianca pulls at Helena's forehead to smooth the lines away.

Bianca
I need . . .
Helena
What?
Bianca
Something.

Gently touching Helena's face.
Thunder.
Sudden dark. Sudden rain.
A wail from Bianca.

Helena
I told you. I told you.

Helena pulls her under the shelter of the arcades and away.
A song. Called and echoed quickly and lightly among the Capulet girls on their balconies.

Alice
Que sentimada.
Others
Que sentimada.
Rhona
Paina.
Others
Paina.
Livia
La Bellina.
Others
La Bellina.
Helena
In la casa.

Others
    In la casa.
Alice
    Dit.
Others
    Dit.
All
    Bertolina.

Suddenly harsh.

Laa laa laa
La la la la la
La la la
La la la
Laaaaa.

It could be 1500; 1900; 2000; or 3000.
    Scaffolding on three sides. An impression of height.
Two irregular levels.
    Rhona and Alice are on the second level.
    Percussion on the ground underneath the
scaffolding.
    Pots of trailing red geraniums on each level.
Opulent pots. Red and green and terracotta.
    Pieces of domestic modernity here and there.
A chrome toaster. A gleaming electric fan. A fridge.
    Here and there, fish bowls full of terrapins.
    In a corner on the ground, a heap of lilies. The
bottom ones dried out. The middle ones rotting. The
top ones fresh.
    Thunder and church bells.
    The rain's pouring down.
    Benvolio's watching from the shadows with
Valentine.
    In the distance, Rosaline.

Benvolio
She's coming back.
Valentine
There's better fish in the sea than ever came out of it.

Benvolio grabs him.

Benvolio
Do you call my love a fish, sir?
Valentine
Do I call your love a fish, sir?
Benvolio
Do you call my love a fish?
Valentine
I do call your love a fish.
Benvolio
Do you call her a fish, sir?
Valentine
I do call her a fish, sir.
I do not call her a trout.
Benvolio
You do not call her a trout, sir?
Valentine
I do not call her a trout, sir.
Do you crush my collar?
Benvolio
I do crush your collar, sir.
Valentine
Do you crush my new collar?
Benvolio
What kind of fish?
Valentine
What kind of fish?
Benvolio
What kind of fish, sir?
Valentine
A red snapper.

Benvolio
  A red snapper?
Valentine
  A red snapper.
Benvolio
  That's a pretty kind of fish.
Valentine
  It is a tasty fish.
  Prettier than a pike.
Benvolio
  Do you call my love a pike?
Valentine
  I do call you a fool.
  Throw your cat fish back in the pond.
  And unhand my lace, Benvolio.

  Misery provoked.

Benvolio
  I haven't got her out of the pond yet.
  She is a young carp.
  Queen of fish, Valentine,
  Who will not come to my hand
  Though I tempt her with soft white bread.
  And I tell her my hand is gentle.
Valentine
  A carp?

  Valentine pouches up his mouth and makes a fish face.

Benvolio
  It was a metaphor.
Valentine
  Fuck off.
Benvolio
  I'm not asking you to love her.
Valentine
  Don't go down this road, Benvolio.

Benvolio
  Will I lose your friendship?
Valentine
  For loving a Capulet?
Benvolio
  Well?
Valentine
  The Prince says hostilities are at an end.
Benvolio
  What do you say?
Valentine
  Can the Prince change the habits of a lifetime with
      a word?
  Did his 'word' bring my brother back to life?
  Do the dead live because an amnesty is called?
  And if they don't live how can there be peace?
      Where is Mercutio now?
  There is such a silence
  In the world
  Since he has left it.
  I was never alone
  Not even in the womb.
  For we were twin souls
  Mercutio and me.
  Now I am cut in half
  My good part's gone.
  His death sets my heart
  To beat a tattoo of hate.
  The Prince may speak his word.
  May speak and speak.
  He cannot change my heart beat.
      I'll watch the girl with you in friendship.
  Approach her and our friendship ends.
Benvolio
  At least it's wet.

Valentine
Why?
Benvolio
Hate cools in the rain.
Tears become invisible.

The drummer hits the rim: points at Valentine.

Valentine
And yet it's close.

He whirrs a small electric hand fan into life.
    The shadows hide them.
    The rain patters down.
    The drum sticks click.
    *Rosaline walks up to a pile of flowers in the corner
of the piazza. She's holding a single lily. And an
umbrella.*

Rosaline
Your spirit haunts me, Juliet.
I see more of you dead
Than I did when you were alive;

Valentine splutters with laughter.
    The drummer whirls and points.
    Benvolio puts his hand over his friend's mouth.

That's a joke.
'More of you dead.'

*She stamps her foot hard down as if knocking on the
door of the grave.*

Go on laugh.
And more of you alive
Than I wanted to.
Laugh. Laugh, go on.

Knocks again.

Come on, Juliet.

Benvolio pulls Valentine deep into the shadows.

We were hardly close as cousins.
You were too small, too pretty, too rich,
Too thin and too much loved for me to cope with.
'Spoilt' is the word that springs to mind
Though I don't want to speak ill of the dead.

*She touches the stamen of the lily. Yellow nicotine
pollen stains her fingers. She rubs it in.*

All a flower does is wither
It's the memories that stay for ever:
So they tell me.
So what do I recall of you?
Juliet, daddy's princess, rich,
Mummy's darling, quite a bitch.
You scratched my face once,
From here to here;
I have the scar. I have it yet.
You can see it quite clearly
In the sunlight;
A silver line.
You wanted my favourite doll.
And of course you got it.
For though I was scarred, you cried.
And your nurse swooped down
And took the moppet from me.
Spanked me hard for making you unhappy;
Gave my doll to you, her dearest baby.
Later you stole my best friend;
Wooed her with whispers;
Told her gossip's secrets;
Gave her trinkets, sweetmeats.
Later still, you took my love
And didn't know you'd done it;

Then having taken him
You let him die.
If you'd swallowed the friar's potion earlier
You would have wakened.
And my love would be alive.
None of this would have happened.
I know you, Juliet.
You hesitated, frightened.
Didn't take the stuff until the dawn.
Wakened too late in the tomb.
   In the night I dream of Romeo.
He's reaching his arms out from the vault.
The poison has him in its hold.
He fills my nights with his longing for life.
Until I am afraid to go to sleep.
For though I love him still
I cannot soothe his pain.
If I could, I would
But it is not me he's reaching for.
   So why, Juliet,
Should I spend my cash
On flowers for you?
Are you a saint
Simply because you were daft enough
To die for love?
Love?
A passing fancy,
No more nor less.
Tomorrow or tomorrow or tomorrow
You would have tired of him.
Like your fancy for the doll;
Once possessed, you left it in the rain;
Yesterday's fancy, mud in its hair,
Damp stained the dress I'd made for her.
   They think you brave to have taken your life
But you believed in immortality.

Daddy's princess could not die.
She would be there at her own funeral
To watch the tears flow
And hear her praises sung.
     So you haunt me.
Don't turn away.
Listen. Listen.
What is it that you've brought about?
What trail does your fancy drag behind?
What punishments lie in your fancy's wake?
Listen, Juliet.
Come here. Come close.
Press your ear to the earth
So I know you're listening.
There's a trial going on.
Even now. In all solemnity.
Four lives hang in the balance
Forced by your selfish suicide
To take their chance
Standing at the mercy of the court.
They wait to see whether life or death
Is granted them by what we call justice.
It's a strange justice. Law meted out by the rich
Who measure their wisdom
By the weight of their gold;
As if riches bear witness to virtue.
You and I know they don't.
So four poor people are brought before the Prince
To see whether they live or die.
You brought this on them.
No feud wrought their trials.
Their misery is tribute
To your precocity.
Married. And at thirteen!
     So. So. Sweet Coz.

Here. This is the last flower
You'll get from me.
Death flowers have the sweetest scent.

She casts the flower down. Shrugs.

That's that bit done.

She puts down the umbrella. Stands with her face up to the rain.

Benvolio
Some loves are for ever.
Valentine
Jealous of dead Juliet.
Oh Lord. Oh Lord.
These Capulets.
Love?
This is love.
A pile of rotting lilies.
Benvolio
They're still fresh on the top.
Valentine
Only you.
Benvolio
What?
Valentine
A pile of stinking lilies bathed in catpiss,
Only you would see the fresh ones on the top.
And love Rosaline whose heart's in the grave.
There are softer beds to lie on
Than fair Rosaline's nail strewn cot.
Benvolio
I love because I love.
I can't say why I love.
I would take her in my arms,
Confess my love,

Ask for her clemency.
Change her name.

Valentine

She'd have you for breakfast.
That girl is the enemy.
She'd eat you up, suck on the bits
And after, lick her chops.
She's a hurt animal.
A cat that would attack the hand
That gentles it.
And bite it hard.
Princess of Cats.
She's a better man
Than Tybalt ever was
Or Petruchio ever shall be.
Give her a sword
She'd show you no mercy.
Though she has no need of a sword.
What woman does?
While the Prince has taken our weapons
He's left them theirs.

Benvolio

What weapons?

Valentine

Have you no sisters?
A woman's weapon is her tongue.
See her. See.
Conjoin with her.
You'll fight the oldest feud of all.
Not Montagues and Capulets.
Men and women Benvolio.
Men and women. There's a war.
Will never end by any decree
Of man, or Prince, or God. Don't go near her.

Valentine mimes whipping out a sword. Mimes
balancing it on the tips of his fingers by its point.

Benvolio
There's no sword there.
Valentine
I see a sword.
A Toledo steel.
My sword.
The hilt thirsty for my hand.
The blade starved of blood.
See it gleam in the light.
See it. See it.

He mimes throwing it up in the air, catching it again
and sheathing it.

Now it's gone.
When the trial's over
And the guilty hung
I'll have my sword again.

The sun gleams out for a moment.
   Light everywhere.
   Below, Lorenzo leans against a pillar. Waiting. He
has a little blue electric fan. It whirrs. He leans and
fans himself. Lethargically. Leaning into the breeze
from the fan. Trying and trying to click the fingers of
the other hand.

Gianni
Tea. There is no point even trying to make it without
first warming the pot. They do it. People do it.
Lemon? Milk? They say, brandishing a cold tea pot.
The question doesn't arise. Why? Why would you
make tea if you hadn't warmed the pot. Once the
pot's warmed, with boiling water mind. Once the
tea's spooned in, dry and black and perfumed with

bergamot. Not blended, no shred of dust. I won't have sweepings from the floor that some chap's relieved himself upon. Once boiling water is added. While waiting in that delicious pause when the tea is giving of its essence. Then the question of lemon or milk can be addressed. With Earl Grey lemon always. But in the winter I would maintain it has to be lemon any way. Whether Darjeeling or Assam; lemon and not milk in the winter. Because. There is always a danger that the milk is contaminated. Turnips. That's the danger. In the winter time. There are those who feed their cows turnips.

Lorenzo

I can't get a click out of my fingers.

Gianni

I can taste the turnip in the milk.

Lorenzo

I'm so hot I can't get my fingers to click. My hands are damp. Slimy to touch. No woman will marry a man with a damp hand.

Gianni

In the tea I can taste a turnip fed cow.
An abomination.
I hope there's no turnips in heaven.
    Suppose they hang them.
Suppose they do that?

Lorenzo

It's not our business.
We're here, Petruchio's men,
Waiting to be counted
To elect him Prince of Cats.

Gianni

Foregone conclusion
No man will stand against him.
    I wouldn't like to hang.
Dying in front of a crowd.

Dancing for their amusement.
Shitting myself. Piss rolling down my leg.
    We've all been to Mantua after all. Saturdays would
never have been Saturdays without his pinks and blues.
The apothecary only served us.

Lorenzo
We paid him, Gianni.

Gianni
We taught him to depend on us.
And we only paid him sometimes.
We kept him on a string.
Rich men have enough to eat.
His pills didn't make him fat.

Lorenzo
He didn't do it for charity.

Gianni
We kept him dangling.
He scraped a living.
Then Romeo comes along.
'You give me poison:
I'll give you forty ducats.'
Like that's a bloody fortune
Like he's going to say no.
Romeo seduced him with his ducats,
Why hang the apothecary?

Lorenzo
They can hardly hang Romeo.
He's saved them the price of the rope.
I'd turn out for that.
To see a Montague hang.

Gianni
The heat and waiting for a man you've known to die.

Lorenzo
It's not decided.

Gianni
Tell me it won't happen.

Tell me.
Even honourable men
Need a scapegoat.

Lorenzo sticks out his tongue. He brings the whirring fan towards it. Gianni watches terrapins. To and fro the fan goes until the tongue's held there on the whirring fan.

A girl standing on a table, Alice. Looking down at Rosaline. Rhona's pinning up her dress. Then tacking the hem.

Alice

My God. My God. What's she got on?
Standing there. Standing in the rain. **

Rhona

Turn.
Turn.

Alice

** I wouldn't wear that.
I wouldn't give that to my servant to wear.
I'd rip it off my mother's back, for God's sake,
If I saw she had it on.
And my mother is not known for her taste.
But that. That beats anything
My mother might buy in a flea market.
She won't come to the election tonight in that?
She'd hardly dare.
Vote Petruchio Prince of Cats?
Put her hand in the air in that?
There's holes in the armpits.

Benvolio pulls Valentine into the shadows as Rosaline goes past.

I know she's unhappy.
We're all unhappy.
I mean look at her. Look at her, Rhona.

She's letting the side down.
She should have more pride.
If she's got to mourn publicly
She could at least do it prettily.
What did she see in Romeo
That our boys don't have?
I wouldn't waste my time.
All this for a dead man.
What can you do with a dead man
When there are live ones waiting
Who can give you some return.

Below. Lorenzo takes the fan away from his tongue.
A couple of hideous sounds. Then tortured speech.

Lorenzo
My tongue is numb.

His words are indistinct.

My tongue is totally . . .
Gianni
Ever seen terrapins doing it?

Lorenzo's prodding his tongue. Squeezing it.

You listening to me?
Lorenzo?
I'm talking to you?
Lorenzo
My tongue's numb.
Gianni
Have you seen a terrapin on the job?

Very slurred.

Lorenzo
Tortoises.
Gianni
I've seen tortoises. They're always humping. Tortoises.

When they're awake they're humping. When they're not eating. When they're not sleeping. Humping. Course it's a slow business.

If I was stuck in a bowl and all I had was another terrapin I'd be doing it. All day I'd be doing it. Every day. In every way.

What did we used to talk about? In the old days? Last week? We had plans last week.

Lorenzo

My tongue is numb. My tongue is numb.

Gianni

I'd kill for a cup of tea.

It's all I've got left to excite me.

They melt away.

The drummer click click clicks his sticks. Points at Rosaline.

She walks away from the flowers.

Alice is craning to see.

Alice

Coming home.

Rhona

Keep still.

You've got St Vitus dance.

Alice

That's a curse.

Take it back.

Say a thing

And you make it so.

Take it back, Rhona.

Rhona

You're a drama queen.

Alice

And you're from Glasgow.

It's a well known fact

Glaswegians
Don't know anything.

Rhona
They know how to kiss.

Alice
Are you threatening me?

Rhona
Keep this up
It'll be Christmas and this dress
Still won't be done.
Forget the election tonight.
Keep this up,
You'll be an old woman;
You'll be dead
And this won't be ready
To be your winding sheet.

Silence.
   Alice shrugs. Stands still.

Alice
One fresh flower, that's all.
Six yesterday.
Ten the day before.
It's falling off.

Rhona
They're all watching the trial.

Alice
I wish we'd gone.

A pin goes into her leg.

That hurt.
What's wrong with you?

Rhona
Gawping at those poor folk,
The crowd counting the tears,

41

Glorying in the thrill
Of watching folk who may be about to die
At the hand of the state.
Nurse calling on her Juliet.
The old man, the friar,
Aged ten years in a day.
Peter, who brought the ladder
Romeo used,
To climb to Juliet's room
Just did as he was told;
Hasn't got a mind of his own;
Hasn't ever had one.
And the apothecary?
I feel sorry for him.
I won't go to the court.
I don't want to pry.

Alice

There's only one life.
You have to find enjoyment where you can.

Silence.

You're such a prude.
Lighten up, Rhona.
What will be, will be
And we can't change a thing,
Cavil we at it ever so.
I've more important things
On my mind than a trial.
I need this dress for the evening's frolic.
I'll dance with our new Prince of Cats.
Later I will marry him.
Not that he knows that.
Nor will he till it's done.
Make the dress fine, Rhona.
I have plans.

Clouds and shadows sweep the alleys.
  A call like a wolf howling. Echoing.
  Another and another. Music.
  Helena has a basket over her shoulder. Loaves and green leaves stick out of it. She has Bianca by the hand.
  Bianca hangs back.
  The drummer whacks a big stick against a scaffolding bar.
  Bianca cowers.

Helena
  Come on.
Bianca
  Dark.
Helena
  Move Bianca. Move. Move.

She tugs but Bianca doesn't move.
  Shadows loom and threaten. Become people.
  The howling closes in. No faces. Flashes of green here and there. Montague colours.
  Helena shelters Bianca with her body.
  Rosaline runs down. She has a stick in her hand. Livia follows her.
  She clacks the stick round the scaffolding uprights. Livia following.
  The Montagues melt away. One stops. Stares at Rosaline. His face caught in a glint of sunlight. Benvolio.
  Valentine pulls him away.
  Bianca whimpers softly.

Rosaline
  What news from the trial?
Helena
  'The nurse of Juliet, is banisht in her age,

43

Because that from the parents she dyd hyde the
    mariage.'

Livia
    Poor Angelica.

Rosaline
    And Peter?

Helena
    No news of him. Nor Friar Lawrence,
    Poor fond old man.

Livia
    The apothecary?

Helena
    Held till last tonight.

Rosaline
    So she lives, the nurse.

Helena
    Than any punishment the Prince could give her,
    The loss of Juliet is the worst.
    Angelica truly loved her.

Livia
    But to leave here and live with strangers.

Helena
    She's allowed till sunset to do her rounds
    And say good-bye.

The drummer whacks the scaffolding with his stick.

Rosaline
    They haven't gone.
    Take her home,
    Take her home.

    Blackout.

Rhona
    Have you a purse I could have?

Alice
    My Spanish leather.

Rhona
Where is it?
Alice
In the drawer.

Alice twirls in her dress. And twirls.

Rhona
It's not done yet.
Alice
This was my bridesmaid's dress
When Juliet was to wed Paris.
Then it was the dress
At her first funeral
When she died the first time
And all we bridesmaids attended her
Supposed corpse.
Then it was at her real funeral.
This dress has a history.
More history than it needs.

She wriggles.

And less décolletage.

On the other balcony.
Helena puts a light cover round Bianca.
Bianca holds her hand.

Bianca
I dreamed.
Helena
Gone now.
Bianca
You left me.
Helena
I'm here.
Bianca
Not in my dream.

Helena
　Who was in your dream?
Bianca
　Juliet.
Helena
　What was she doing?
Bianca
　She was waiting.
　'Do you want me?' I said.
　I wasn't stupid in my dream.
　Juliet didn't say anything.
　Didn't move. Went on waiting.

*Helena wipes tears from Bianca's face with the heel of
her hand.*

Helena
　They've gone now. You're safe.
　They won't touch you.
　I won't let them.
Bianca
　If you're stupid, Helena,
　Why do you have to know it?
　No man will ever love me.
　I'll have no child to call my own.
　Any man would feel demeaned
　By my hand on his arm.
　I was like you in my dream.
　I liked me.
Helena
　Do you still see her?
Bianca
　When this day ends Juliet will go.
　But she won't be alone.
　The barriers are all coming down
　Between her land and ours.
　And I'm frightened.

You won't cross over, Helena?

Helena
I won't cross over.

Bianca
Promise.

Helena
I won't leave you.

Bianca
When will the day be done?

Helena
When we have a new Prince of Cats,
When Friar Lawrence knows his fate
And the apothecary.

Bianca
Will the rain ever stop?

Helena
I don't know.

Bianca
Sing me.

Helena
What?

Bianca
Sing me the hunchback song.

Helena
Aren't you hungry?

Bianca
Sing me.

Helena curls up with Bianca.

Helena
** Gobba la madre,
Gobbo il padre
Gobba la figlia di sua sorella. *

Bianca
His sister's daughter was a hunchback.

Helena
* Gobba anchi quella *
Bianca
They were all hunchbacks.
Helena
Gobba anchi quella.
Gobba la madre,
Gobbo il padre,
Gobba la figlia di sua sorella
Gobba anchi quella.
La familla Gobbetin
Gobba anchi quella
La familla Gobbetin.

** *There's a load of stuff in the drawer. Rhona finds the purse.*

Rhona
We'll fill it.
She'll need money.
Alice
Who?
Rhona
The nurse, Alice.
For her journey.
Alice
Spanish leather
For Angelica.
Take the other.
Here.
Rhona
It's threadbare.
Alice
So much the better.
And don't give her too much money.
Over generous charity
Only encourages idleness.

For her own good
Limit your kindness.
Nurse was after all a little less
Than wise.

Rhona

She's punished then.

Alice

I would have had her hanged.

Rhona

You'd make heaven cold.
With your philosophy.

Alice

I'm not good like you;
I'm just marking time;
Idling in chatter gear,
Because the world's changed.
It's standing still;
The clouds in the sky unmoving.
The world's in shadow;
Before it was fraught with light.
Now there's a glooming chiaroscuro
Over all. And I feel evil inside.
Why did they do this thing
To my world?
I wanted it to stay as it was
Charged with energy
Till I grew up
And joined it;
Some man's mistress.
Some warrior's Queen.
So hang them all
Who broke the world
Where I was happy.
Why should they live?
Who raped my dream.
Don't look at me like that.

Do you have to try to be good
Or does it come naturally?
    You were always grown up.
Glasgow's a dark place
I've heard it said.
It grows dour people
Steeped in fear.
Statistically
There are far more suicides there
Than we have here.

Rhona

You look nice.

She puts thread and scissors in the drawer.
    Alice shrugs the dress down to give herself more
of a cleavage. Pushes her breasts up.

Alice

When Petruchio is elected Prince of Cats
He'll not look past me.

Rhona

You'll have your nipples hanging out
Any minute now.

Alice

Some women tattoo round their nipples.
And their actual nipples
They tattoo those too.
I'd quite like blue nipples.
That would be
Decadent.
Something to show my
Grandchildren
When I'm old,
To bear witness to a wild youth.
Chance would be a fine thing.
I'm just waiting to grow old;
Standing here waiting to grow old;

I'm older with every breath I take.
Nothing ever happens
Any more.
I feel time passing,
Every second of it heavy.
I'll have blue tattoos on my nipples
So I've got something to show.

Drum sticks click.
  Alice looks at the drummer.
  Nods.

She can have my leather purse.
I'm not as mean
As you deem me.
I was born a bitch.
It'll take a lifetime
To overcome it.

Rosaline's at the mirror changing into boy's clothes.

Rosaline
  What is love?
  Answer me.
  A couple of sighs in the night.
  A rhythmic expiration.
  Slightly voiced.
  As in
  Ah ah.
  Or
  Mmm mm mm.
  A quick thrust of time
  And it's over.
    Love is not carried on an evening's zephyr breeze.
  Love is not in the pulsed scent of a woman's cologne.
  Love is not in the turn of a man's head;
  In his shadowed profile

In the laugh that you hear unawares;
In the gentle brush of his hand on your skin.
    Love is only the rut
A quick pant and it's gone. **

Alice
    Five times she's said love
    In five breaths.
    And you think I have a one-track mind.
Rona
    Where's the money?
Alice
    In the jar.

Rosaline
    ** If love maintains
    That's the desire
    To rut again.
Livia
    I liked you
    How you used to be.
Rosaline
    Something happened
    I grew up suddenly.
Livia
    Benvolio's looking for you.
Rosaline
    After what he's done?
Livia
    He was trying to stop them.
Rosaline
    It's never going to end, Livia.

    A beat.

Livia
You could look back at him.
It's only polite.
Rosaline
Three of our family are killed by his family.
It's never going to end.

She buckles on an empty scabbard.

Livia
What are you doing?

The drummer click click clicks. Rosaline nods.

Rosaline
The Gods want war.
Livia
Where are you going?
Rosaline
To even the score.
Livia
Romeo's mother died the night of his banishment,
Died of a broken heart.
Rosaline
That doesn't count.
   We need weapons, Livvy.
Will you come?
Livia
Where are you going?
Rosaline
The tomb.
Livia
Why?
Rosaline
So the men can lend me their honour
For the honour of all Capulets.
Livia
You're as bad as they are.

Pause.

Rosaline
I'll go alone.

She climbs down.
Benvolio stares from the shadows. Smiles.

Don't be nice to me.
I don't want you to be nice.
Benvolio
I'm sorry.
Rosaline
What for?

As they're talking, Gianni and Lorenzo set up a trip
wire.

Benvolio
What happened down there
With Bianca.
Before.
Won't happen again.
Rosaline
I know it won't.
I'll make sure it won't.
Benvolio
I'm sorry.
Rosaline
That's easy said.
Benvolio
It's not Bianca you care about.
Rosaline
Sorry's just a word.
Benvolio
Whatever you do
You're not doing it for Bianca.
Rosaline
Why else am I doing it?

Pause.

Benvolio
Romeo.
Rosaline
Alive
I could have fought to regain his love.
I could have fought
I would have won.
A heart that's fickle and can turn
Would be fickle still
And turn again.
Benvolio
As well he's dead then.
Rosaline
He was your cousin
And your friend.
Benvolio
As well he's dead for you.
If he'd been alive;
If you'd fought for his love;
If you'd won;
If you'd married then
Your whole long life
You would have spent
Wondering if this one
Or that one
Had taken his butterfly fancy.
I loved him as a brother.
But as well he's dead;
I wouldn't have that life for you,
Smelling his discarded clothes
For another woman's perfume.
What would he have driven you to?
I love you, Rosaline,
I'll not play around.

He touches her face so gently. And for a moment she
lets him, responds even. Almost nuzzling her cheek
into his palm.
  The drummer click, click, clicks. Rosaline backs off.

Rosaline
  You promise a whole lot more
  Than you can deliver.
Benvolio
  Test me.

She's about to speak.
  The drummer points.
  Rosaline runs.

Rosaline. Rosaline. Rosaline.

He begins to run after her.

Lorenzo
  Now.

The string's pulled. Benvolio falls.
  Gianni pinions his arms.

Gianni
  What have we here?
Lorenzo
  By his smell
  A Montague.
Benvolio
  Peace.
  Let me go.
Lorenzo
  'Let me go.'
Benvolio
  In the Prince's name.
Lorenzo
  'In the Prince's name.'

Benvolio
For the sake of the truce.
Lorenzo
He wants us to let him go.
Gianni
Make him ask nicely.
Lorenzo
What kind of nicely?
Benvolio
I have to . . .
Lorenzo
Quiet. Gianni's thinking;
Looking for a form of words
That would satisfy him
A Montague has some manners.

Benvolio struggles.

If I were you I would not struggle.
Gianni might think you were an agent
Come to spoil our ritual
When we make our Prince of Cats.
Then he would not be merciful.
** Escalus may have our swords,
There are other weapons,
A shard of glass
Will slice a throat.
* Handily
A stone may break a head.

* *He picks up a stone. Raises it.*
   ** *The Nurse with all her bags rounds the side of the arcade.*
   Takes in the scene. Dumps her bag. Runs at the boys.

Nurse
It is enough.

It is enough
Is it not enough?
Lorenzo, Gianni.
I want you here.
By me.
No more mischief.
Or I'll speak what I know of you.
Long tales of night fears and bed wetting,
To beguile the ears of a Montague.
Come now. Let him go.
And kiss your nurse.
Bid her farewell
Send her on her road.
I said my good-byes to your parents at the court.
Come down to me.
All the cousins of my Juliet
Who were to be her bridesmaids
But strewed wedding flowers round her tomb instead;
Come to me,
For I won't see you in this life again.
Not after this night.

The girls begin to climb down.
   Benvolio slides into the shadows. Runs after
Rosaline.

I don't see Rosaline.
Where is she, Livvy?
Alice that dress is much too low.
Rhona talk some sense into her,
She doesn't need to advertise her wares
So brazenly.
She can leave something to the imagination
And still hook Petruchio.
When do you go home?

Rhona
   When the trial's over

And life has settled down.
My aunt needs me to mind the house.
While she's at the court.
Please take this purse from Alice.

Nurse
My kind, sweet girl.

Alice
It's not just from me.
It's from Rhona too.

Nurse
Where's Helena?

Helena
Here. I've brought you a coat.
We had one to spare.

Nurse
Bring my Bianca to me.
My little love.

Helena pushes Bianca forward.
  The dream's in her eyes.
  She's far far away.

Livia
What news from the court?

Nurse
'Peter, for he did obey his master's hest
In wonted freedom has good leave to lead his lyfe
    in rest.'
One day he says. He may follow me.
I look forward to that day.
Petruchio's not here.
Nor Rosaline.
The sun sinks faster in this square than it would on
    a hill.

Silence.

Feel the quiet.
Smell it.
Time to go.

Petruchio runs in.

Petruchio
I thought I had missed you.
Nurse
Look after them.
You're a good man.
I charge you to keep to the peace.
I charge you, Petruchio.
Petruchio
I swear.
Nurse
Tell Rosaline.
Tell her I love her.
Say Angelica was here.

She picks up her bags.

Don't follow.
No more good-byes.
See the sun.
Glimmering out
From a low cloud.
See. See now –
The sun dies.

A moment.
    And she's gone.

Lorenzo
I declare Petruchio
Prince of Cats in his brother's place.
Petruchio
Not yet.
We're not all here.

Gianni
No man stands against you.
Petruchio
Even so.
We'll wait until we are all gathered.
Alice that is a very fetching gown.
Alice
An old thing
It's hard to dress well
When in mourning.
I'm glad you like it,
Petruchio.

The drummer clicks his sticks and points at Bianca.
Juliet and Bianca speak in chorus.

Bianca/Juliet
'Don't touch him.'
Helena
Bianca!
Bianca/Juliet
'Don't let her.
He's mine.'
Livia
Juliet?

The drummer clicks.
    Light on Rosaline in the tomb.
    Taking Romeo's hand.

Bianca/Juliet
'She takes his hand.
Moves his cold fingers
One by one,
Makes him cup her warm cheek.
His palm warms at her touch.
And now she cradles him.'

Petruchio
Hold her.
Bianca/Juliet
'My one and only love.
My night and day.
In the moonlight I kissed his skin.
His skin in the silver moonlight.
Don't let her take the taste of my lips from his mouth.
Please. Please. Please.'

Helena's trying to hold her.

Alice
Who is she looking at? * *
What does she see?
Rhona
* * She sounds like Juliet.
Bianca/Juliet
'Tell her no.
Tell her don't.
Tell her don't come near me.'

Drums.
  Blackout.
  In the tomb.
  A single source of light. Not quite steady.
  A small voice of panic.

Rosaline
I thought they'd taken you.
I thought they'd taken your bodies.
I thought they'd taken you away.
The Prince said . . .
I wouldn't have come . . .
The Prince said to take you from the vault,
Lie you together in your own tomb
Where we laid the flowers.

The Prince said . . .
'Lest that length of time might from our myndes
   remove,
The memory of so perfect, sound, and so approved
   love.'

Then she creeps close.

And is this love?
Her head on your shoulder.
Your arm around her.
And is this death?
Death it must be.
Sleep has a gentler air.
I watched my mother die.
But this is different.
Colder.
Sore.
   She washed your mind clean.
You didn't ever think of me.
Never once thought of me.
And I loved you so.
But being unloved
I am not allowed sorrow.
I am not allowed a widow's tears.
   You look like strangers.

A cymbal crash.
   Blackout.
   *A match is struck. Valentine holds it. A small glow
in the quite, quite dark. Rosaline's light moves to and
fro below.*
   Benvolio moves through the gloom. Trips. A curse.

Valentine
   Shhhhh.

*Another match struck on a tinder box. He lights a
hurricane lamp.*

Benvolio
Where have you been?
Valentine
Where are you going?
Benvolio
I asked you first.
Valentine
I've been at the court.
Benvolio
'What shall betide of the grey-bearded syre?
Of fryre Lawrence thus araynde, that good barefooted
    fryre?'
Valentine
'Because that many times he woorthely did serve
The common welth, and in his lyfe was never found
    to swerve,
He is discharged quyte, and no marke of defame
Must seeme to blot, or touch at all, the honor of
    his name.'
But he's taking himself to a hermitage.
To live quite alone.
In silence and contemplation.
He leaves his simples behind.
He takes no papers on which to write,
He takes no inks, no pens.
He will not mark down his knowledge.
For his knowledge killed.
He will communicate with no man.
The court having shown him mercy and respect
He has decreed his own punishment.
No wine will cross his lips.
No food but dry bread.

He will look at the world through a narrow aperture
  in a brick wall.
Benvolio
  A living death.
Valentine
  But for him, he says,
  Romeo and Juliet would be alive.
Benvolio
  So is it over?
Valentine
  But for the apothecary.
  They still sit in judgement.

Valentine unsheathes his sword.
  Lays it on the earth.

Benvolio
  You have your sword.
Valentine
  Not mine. Still she is beautiful.
Benvolio
  It is like yours.
Valentine
  My brother's sword.
  I have one for you.
Benvolio
  How have you your brother's sword?
Valentine
  He lent it to me.
  I promised him I would give it back.
    The one yours came from
  Had lost his head;
  And having no lips
  Was reluctant to vouchsafe his name,
  Which though I asked most cordially,
  He didn't have the heart to answer.

Still it's a fine piece.
The donor was a little stiff.
He had no further need of it.
I promise you.

Benvolio

You spoke with your brother?

Valentine

I did most of the talking
In all honesty.
I promised him
A death
So he could rest easy.

Benvolio

You went down into the tomb?
This is madness, Valentine.

Valentine

I'm not the only one mad.

The light below them wavers and wavers.
    Rosaline climbs up onto a level with them. She's carrying a bundle.
    Valentine claps his hand over Benvolio's mouth. Shades the lantern.
    Rosaline turns. Sees nothing. Her light bobs away. Valentine lets the lamp glow again.

It seems we'll have some fun tonight.

A cymbal crash.
    Blackout.
    Bright candlelight.
    Rosaline unrolls her bundle. Swords clank out and lie gleaming dully in the night.

Petruchio

Illegal weapons?

Rosaline

What do you bring, Petruchio?

Petruchio
This is an election.

Rosaline
It precedes a war.

Petruchio
It precedes a peace.

Rosaline
So you say.

Petruchio
Your clothes don't make a man of you.

Rosaline
I wear the clothes to fight more easily.
I have no wish to be a man.

Petruchio
Are you challenging me?

Rosaline
There is nothing says a woman cannot be leader.
We've had women before.

Petruchio
A social role.

Rosaline
Our laws do not define the position by gender.
Prince or Princess they state.

Petruchio
Why, Rosaline?

Rosaline
Do the Montagues allow peace?
Helena tell him.
I don't want peace.

Petruchio
I do.

Rosaline
Why?
Why?
Look at us.

Without weapons
What will we become?

Petruchio

I'd like to see.

Rosaline

And when you've seen
When you've seen
And we are all ordinary
And we have no purpose.
What then? It'll be too late to turn back.
We'll be out of the fighting way.
What tales then will we tell our children?
We'll have no more heroes,
We'll die old and wrinkled in our beds.
Love will be less sharp.

Petruchio

It wasn't one of us you loved.

Rosaline

I don't want to see our race decline.
Where will our poetry come from,
Hate ironed out of our souls,
Our fighting days done?
Blossom is more sweet today
If death comes tomorrow.

Petruchio

I want to watch the blossom bud;
I want to watch it flower;
I want to watch it fall;
A snow shower of petals on the ground;
And see the buds break next year too.
And the next.
And the next.
And taste the wine
From vines yet to be planted.

I want that for all of us.
Capulets and Montagues.
Rosaline
You want to play boules in the sunshine
Old before your time?
Petruchio
I want to live:
You want to die
And join Romeo in the vault.
And you want to take us with you.
These weapons are chill, Rosaline,
The cold sweat of the grave is on them.

He throws a sword. She catches it.

In a May time. Blossom on the trees.
Perfume in the air. I put a sword in a girl's hand.
Watched her catch up her skirts and fight.
Teasing me. Laughing at me.
The immortal passado I taught her
The punto reverso, the hay.
Rosaline
You know I can fight then
Having taught me yourself.
You all know I can fight.
Petruchio
Can you govern?
Alice
You loved her then, Petruchio?

*She hits Petruchio. Hits him again and again so that
he has to catch her hands.*

You loved Rosaline?
You loved her?
Rosaline
Can you govern, Petruchio?

Laughter.

Petruchio
The Prince has decreed peace.

Rosaline
Peace? I don't know what to do with it.

Alice
Petruchio?

Rosaline
There will be killings anyway
To fill up the space in our minds
Wrought by this Prince-ordained peace.
They'll seem accidental.
But they won't be.
   Better to play by the old rules.
Control the foot soldiers.
Give them discipline.

Alice
Do you still love her?

Livia
Juliet will have died for nothing.

Rosaline
Do you think she had us on her mind
When she wakened in the tomb?
Or peace? You all knew Juliet.
She was a kitten who lived for pleasure.
Only the very fortunate die for something.
   We have a cause.
We still have that.

Petruchio
We don't like them,
They don't like us.
Should they die for it?
Should we?
Because they pierce their daughter's ears at birth
And that's not our practice

Should we die?
Should they?

Rosaline

A heart has only so many beats in it.

Livia

He's right, Rosaline.
You're wrong.

Rosaline

Then your vote goes to him.
Lorenzo?

Lorenzo

I prefer a plain scabbard
To a jewelled one.
A jewelled scabbard
Is good to look at
And promises a great deal
But it's doomed to disappoint.

Rhona

Just like a man.

Lorenzo picks at the pile of weapons.

Lorenzo

A plain scabbard
Is all discovery,
Is what you will,
A plain scabbard
Will last a lifetime.
The other is best at the beginning
Then loses its glitter
As the years go by.

He weighs a weapon in his hand.

Still a jewelled scabbard
Is better than an empty one.
I'll join Rosaline.

Rosaline
 Gianni?
Rhona
 He doesn't have a mind of his own,
 He'll follow his friend.

She flings a sword. Gianni catches it.

Gianni
 I don't want peace, Rhona.
 I've seen old men.
 They don't look happy to me.
 I look better young than I would old.
 And I want to be a pretty corpse
 So the girls garnish me with rose petals
 And bathe me in tears.
Petruchio
 Tears and pathos, Gianni,
 Is that your style?
Gianni
 Pipe and slippers, Petruchio,
 Is that yours?
Petruchio
 You have two, Rosaline.
 I have one.
 Alice?
Alice
 Petruchio?
Petruchio
 Will you stand with me?
Alice
 What do you think?
Petruchio
 Your face is pale.
Alice
 I wonder why.

Petruchio
Stand with me, Alice.
Alice
I don't like to see a man sitting around.
Peace makes men fat. Slender, lean men
Taut with excitement, that's how I like them.
    I never thought I'd follow a woman, Petruchio.
See. I just want things back the way they were before.

She touches his face. And moves to Rosaline.

Petruchio
Rhona?
Rosaline
She has no vote
Being a visitor here.
Rhona
I'm still a Capulet.

A moment. Rosaline nods.

At home in Glasgow
We have ice-cream wars
Amongst other things.
It all seems stupid to me.

Rhona walks to Petruchio's side.

Rosaline
Three to two, Petruchio.
Petruchio
Helena?
Rosaline
They came at you this afternoon.
Helena
Boys calling names.

She walks to Petruchio's side.

Three all.

Holds out her hand to Bianca.

Bianca?

Bianca sucks her thumb.

Come here. Come on.
Then Petruchio's won.
Livia
She's in a dream, Helena.
Helena
Bianca.

The drummer click click clicks.
Rosaline calls and throws a sword.

Rosaline
Bianca?

A muffled drum roll.
A reflex makes Bianca catch the sword.

Helena
Bianca.

Bianca turns to her sister.

Rosaline
That's my sword, Bianca.
Give it to me.

She holds out her hand.

Give it to me.
Helena
Bianca.

The drums stop.
In the silence the drummer takes Bianca by the
hand. Leads her to Rosaline. Bianca hands Rosaline
the sword.

Rosaline

Sit by me.

Petruchio

Is this how your rule begins?

Suborning the innocent?

Rosaline

We were all innocent.

We were all suborned.

Petruchio

I say we can choose.

Rosaline

We've chosen, Petruchio.

As you see.

Petruchio

This feud began not in our father's time

But in our father's father's.

Some small difference began it. This ancient grudge.

In all the tales our mothers tell.

I never heard what was the root cause.

Was it some slight. Some preferment.

Even some small argument between women.

He shrugs.

And yet our young men die.

In the service of this fierce fate

Which Rosaline believes gives our lives meaning.

Rosaline stands.

Rosaline

I don't know where the beginning was.

She puts her hand on her sword hilt.

Here and now. I take the end on me.

The drummer clicks his sticks. Points. Petruchio and the others climb back up to the balconies.

Rosaline waits.
Valentine enters with his sword drawn.
He sees a figure waiting. Only a tall shadow.
He can't tell that it's a girl at all.

Valentine
Will you fight Petruchio?

Rosaline draws her sword.
She's light on her feet. A teasing swordswoman.
In and out of the shadows.
She nicks Valentine's eyebrow.
The blood runs into his eye.
Scattered applause. Light as rain.
Rosaline withdraws.

Rosaline
Wipe the blood from your eye.
Valentine
Rosaline?
Rosaline
I have a scarf here you can borrow.
Bind your head. Staunch the flow.

She holds out a scarf to him. He dabs at the wound.

I don't fight blind men.
Valentine
I don't fight women, Rosaline.
Rosaline
Afraid you might lose, Valentine?
Valentine
I challenge the Prince of Cats.
Rosaline
She salutes you.

Rosaline clashes her sword on his.
He defends.

76

Valentine
I won't fight a woman.

She presses him hard.
He defends.
He has to cut her to save himself.
She falters slightly.

Valentine
Enough.
Rosaline
No.
Valentine
Enough, Rosaline.

She strikes his blade hard.

Rosaline
You didn't say 'please'.
Valentine
There's no honour in this.
Rosaline
There is for me.
Valentine
Stop this fight.

He appeals to the spectators.

Petruchio.

Petruchio moves.
The drummer points. Petruchio freezes.
Rosaline strikes Valentine's sword.

Rosaline
Dozy.

He has to fight.
Benvolio runs in.

77

Benvolio
Stop this.
One of you.
Livia?
Petruchio?

He walks round the spectators.
  Again there is a small movement. Again the drummer freezes it.

The world would be a better place
If it was peopled by cowards.

He puts himself in between Rosaline and Valentine.

Rosaline, the stars are in the sky,
The world is drenched
In the scent of orange blossom.
Put up your sword.
Valentine
The woman is a tigress,
She will never stop.

Rosaline's at him again.

Rosaline
I'll hurt you, Benvolio,
If you come between us.
Benvolio
Would you hurt me?
Would you hurt me?
  Valentine, I'll take your place.
You require a death.
I'll be your champion.
  Rosaline, you require a death,
I'll be your opponent.
I'll fight you.
  Stand back, Valentine.

Benvolio strikes Valentine's sword.

Valentine. Stand away.

Takes his place.
Benvolio and Rosaline fight.
With one hand Benvolio unfastens his jacket.

Rosaline
What are you doing?

They're both breathless.

Benvolio
Making it easy for you.
Giving you clear sight of the target.
Rosaline
Don't patronise me.

He drops his guard deliberately.

Benvolio
Come on, Rosaline. Come on.
I first saw you in the street
In a green dress,
Pale, pale green.
You laughed, Rosaline,
Before the colour was forbidden, yes.
And I turned my head smiling
At the music of your laugh
And the light in your eyes.
You were happy.
Do you still have the dress?
I'd like to see you in that dress.
It was springtime.
Rosaline
You said you'd fight me.
You said you'd fight.
Put up your guard.
Put it up.

He opens his arms wide.

Do you think I won't cut you.
Do you think I won't.

He takes her sword tip and puts it against his skin.

Benvolio
Cut me, then.

A long moment.

Cut me, Rosaline.

Quietly.

Rosaline
No.

She lets the sword tip drop.

You win.

Sheathes it.

Benvolio
Did you love him so much?

They're close. He touches her cheek.
  A moment.
  She turns away.

Rosaline
Have your cats, Petruchio,
I hope they purr for you.

Pause.

Benvolio
That's it.
Valentine
Is it?

Benvolio
Put your weapon down.

A beat.
  Valentine sheathes his sword.
  Rhona's flute.
  The people on the balconies fade into the shadows.

Do you still have the dress?
Rosaline
Yes.
Benvolio
Will you put it on for me?

The moon is bright. Shadows flutter across it. Chase and chase again.

One day?

He takes her hand. Twines his fingers in hers.

Rosaline
In the spring.

But she doesn't smile at him.

Benvolio
Is that a promise?
Rosaline
Maybe.

She isn't close to him. Though she doesn't take her hand away.
  The drummer makes the high hat kiss-kiss.

Alice
So you like a woman who fights.
Petruchio
I never betrayed you.

Alice
What was there to betray?
We made no promises,
You and me,
Save a look here
A touch there.
Petruchio
As long as we have things clear between us.
Alice
Things are clear. Very, very clear
To me at least.
You like a woman who fights.

She hits him on the arm. Hits and hits again. A wind-mill of hitting.

So fight. Come on fight.
Fight, fight, fight.

He holds her arms tight against her.

That's not fair.
Petruchio
Shhh. Sh. Sh.

He kisses her.
  Rhona's flute lilts and haunts.

Lorenzo
That's a sad sound.
Gianni
Sad enough.
Lorenzo
A man could dance his last to that tune.
Gianni
The night's uneasy.
Lorenzo
What do we do now?

Gianni
  I don't know. What do we do?
Lorenzo
  I asked you first.
Gianni
  I asked you second.
Lorenzo
  What now though?
Gianni
  I don't know what now.

Lorenzo stares into a bowl of terrapins. Speaks on a long, long sigh.

Lorenzo
  Terrapins.

Gianni stares down into the night.
  Helena has her arms round Bianca.

Bianca
  'The apothecary high is hanged by the throte,
  And for the paynes he took with him, the hangman
    had his cote.'
  The trial is over
  Night has come.
    Juliet waited and waited.
  Now she's gone.
  The barriers are up again.
  The dream is done.

The drummer tick ticks with his drum sticks.
  The flute plays.
  Two Capulets, one Montague are left on stage.
  Valentine's leaning. Looking up at Gianni looking down. Catches his eye.
  Gianni tugs on Lorenzo's sleeve. They both fix on Valentine.

Valentine pats his sword hilt. Raises an eyebrow in question. Slightly lifts the sword out of the scabbard.

Gianni nods. Accepts the challenge.

He and Lorenzo jump down.

Valentine unsheathes his sword. Wipes it on his jacket.

Waits.

The drummer points.

Lorenzo and Gianni draw their swords.

The flute trills and falls silent.

Blackout.

Online Resources for Secondary Schools and Colleges

To support the use of *Connections* plays in the Drama studio and the English classroom, extensive resources are available exclusively online. The material aims not only to make the most of new technologies, but also to be accessible and easy to use

Visit *www.connectionsplays.co.uk* for activities exploring each of the plays in a wide range of categories

- Speaking and Listening
- Writing
- Reading and Response
- Practical Drama
- Plays in Production
- Themes

Carefully tailored tasks – whether for KS3, KS4 or A-Level – are accompanied by clear learning objectives; National Curriculum links; ideas for extension and development, and for differentiation; Internet links; and assessment opportunities

The material has been compiled by a team of practising English and Drama teachers, headed by Andy Kempe, author of *The GCSE Drama Coursebook* and (with Lionel Warner) *Starting with Scripts: Dramatic Literature for Key Stages 3 & 4*

STANLEY THORNES